SUPER
SURPRISING
TRiViA
ABOUT
SPACE and the
UNIVERSE

by Ailynn Collins

CAPSTONE PRESS
a capstone imprint

Spark is published by Capstone Press, an imprint of Capstone
1710 Roe Crest Drive, North Mankato, Minnesota 56003
capstonepub.com

Library of Congress Cataloging-in-Publication Data is available on
the Library of Congress website.
ISBN: 9781669050353 (library binding)
ISBN: 9781669071716 (paperback)
ISBN: 9781669050315 (ebook pdf)

Summary: Think you know a lot about space and the universe? Prepare
to know even more about amazing galaxies, stars, planets, and space
exploration. You'll be surprised by how much you'll discover in this totally
terrific book of space trivia.

Editorial Credits
Editor: Erika L. Shores; Designer: Heidi Thompson; Media Researcher:
Jo Miller; Production Specialist: Tori Abraham

Image Credits
Getty Images: alex-mit, 29 (bottom); NASA, Cover (bottom left, bottom
right, top right), Cory Huston, 26 (top), CXC/MIT/F.K. Baganoff et al.,
13, Eric Bordelon, 23, ESA, 5, ESA/CSA/STScI, 29 (top), Johns Hopkins
University Applied Physics Laboratory/Southwest Research Institute, 19
(top), JPL, 20, 28, JPL-Caltech, 18-19, JPL-Caltech/R. Hurt (SSC/Caltech),
11, JPL/California Institute of Technology, 12; Science Source: LYNETTE
COOK, 15, New York Public Library, 22, R Jay GaBany/Stocktrek Images,
14; Shutterstock: banderlog, 6, Crystal Eye Studio, 9 (top), Denis Belitsky,
10, Dotted Yeti, 21, Hollygraphic, (design element) throughout, mexrix,
(background) throughout, Mike Ver Sprill, Cover (top left), Nepster, 17
(top), Pixel-Shot, 4, Vectomart, 8, Vladimir Arndt, 16-17, Vytautas Kielaitis, 9
(bottom), Wittybear, 7 (top), Zakharchuk, 7 (bottom); Wikimedia: NASA, 24,
25, 26 (bottom), 27

TABLE OF CONTENTS

Words in **bold** are in the glossary.

DID YOU KNOW?

The universe is only made of two things. **Matter** and **energy**. We can only see a small part of it. Planets and stars make up the part we can see. Most of space is dark matter and energy. These are invisible! What else might surprise you about space?

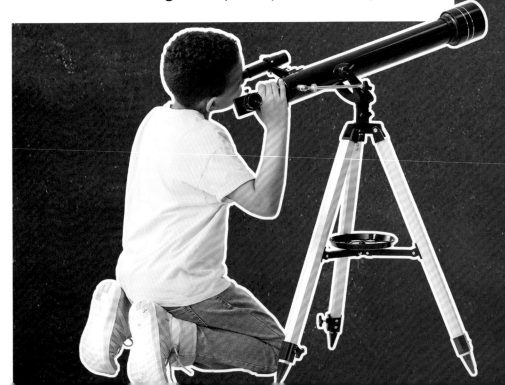

SPACE and the UNIVERSE

The universe began with a big bang 13.8 **billion** years ago. It's getting bigger every day.

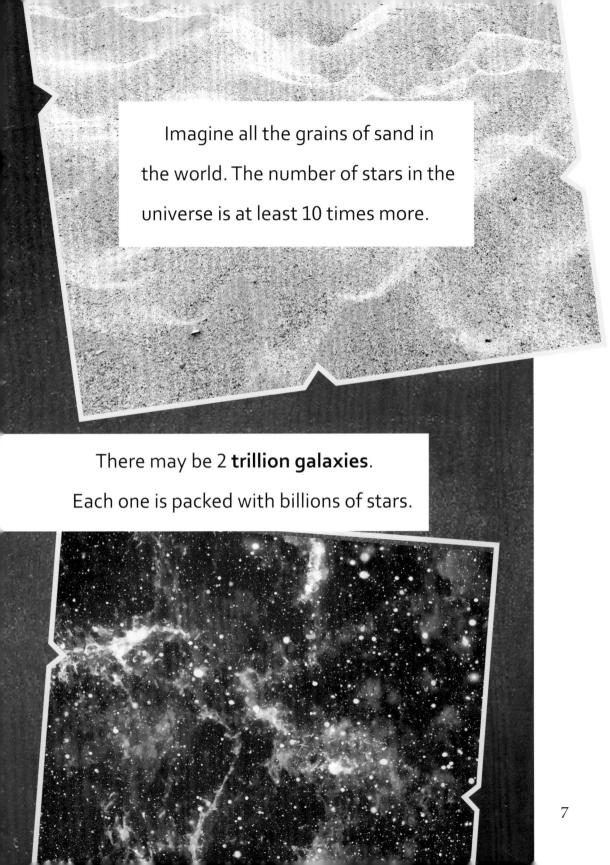

Imagine all the grains of sand in the world. The number of stars in the universe is at least 10 times more.

There may be 2 **trillion galaxies**.

Each one is packed with billions of stars.

Light takes time to travel. If you circled Earth seven and a half times in one second, you'd be traveling at light speed.

The closest star to ours is
Proxima Centauri. Its light takes
more than four years to reach Earth.

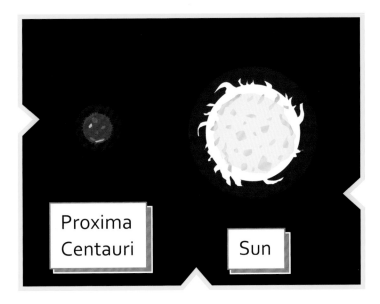

Proxima
Centauri

Sun

The brightest star in our night sky is Sirius.

Its light takes eight years to reach us.

THE GALAXIES

Our galaxy is called the Milky Way. It has more than 400 billion stars. Our Sun is one of them.

Imagine traveling at the speed of light.

It would take you 200,000 years to cross

the Milky Way.

The galaxy nearest to us is Andromeda. Traveling at 10 miles per second, it would take 40 billion years to get there.

In the middle of every galaxy is a **supermassive black hole**. The one in the middle of ours could hold 4 million Suns.

Our galaxy has about 100 million black holes.

In 5 billion years, the Milky Way could crash into the Andromeda galaxy. It would make a bigger galaxy.

When galaxies crash, they can
move up to 2,500 miles per second.

OUR SOLAR SYSTEM NEIGHBORHOOD

Our Sun was called Sol by the Romans long ago. That's how the solar system got its name.

The Sun is 109 times wider than Earth. How many Earths could fit into the Sun? 1,300,000!

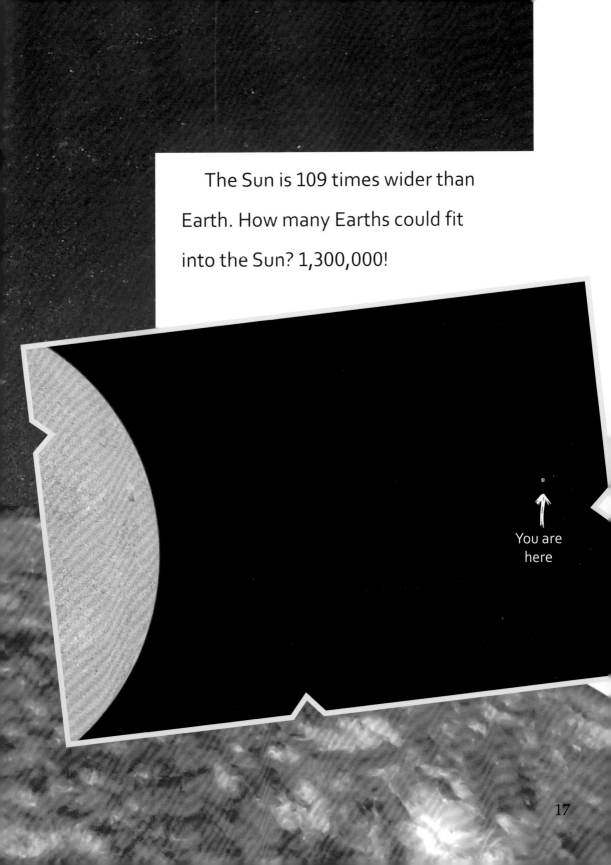

You are here

Venus has more than 1,600 volcanoes. That's the most of all planets in the solar system. Earth has 1,350.

The **dwarf planet** Pluto is very far away. The Sun looks like a bright dot in its sky.

Mars has the tallest mountain of all our planets. Olympus Mons is two and a half times taller than Mount Everest.

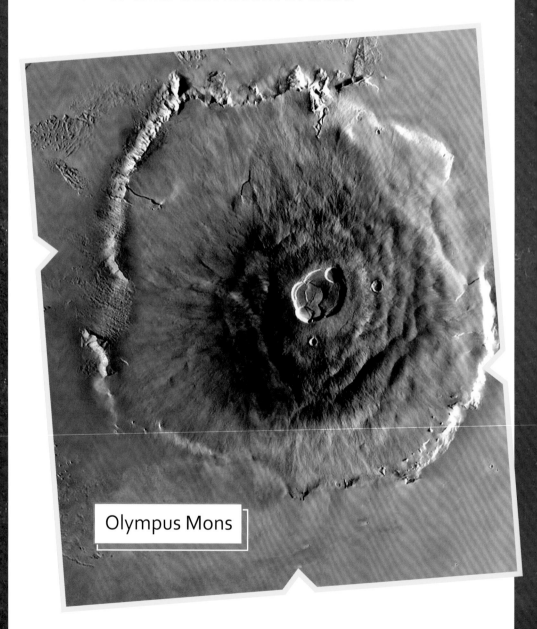

Olympus Mons

You cannot walk on Jupiter, Saturn, Uranus, or Neptune. They don't have a solid surface.

Uranus

Neptune

Jupiter

Saturn

Which planet has the most moons, Jupiter or Saturn? Scientists keep finding new ones. So far, Jupiter has 80. Saturn has 83.

Animals sent into space include monkeys, a chimpanzee, dogs, spiders, jellyfish, and shrimp.

Miss Baker, a squirrel monkey, went into space and came back alive in 1959.

Astronauts are going back to the Moon. These **missions** are called Artemis. Artemis I went without humans, to be sure it was safe.

Artemis I

Artemis III will put the first woman and the first person of color on the Moon.

Buzz Aldrin was the first person to pee on the Moon. He peed into a bag inside his spacesuit.

Mark Vande Hei lived 355 days on the International Space Station (ISS). That's the longest any American has stayed in space at once.

Vegetables are grown on the ISS.
Astronauts on board eat local!

Trash left on the Moon includes two golf
balls, 12 pairs of boots, and 96 bags of poop.

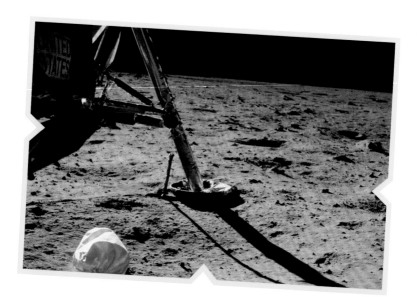

The Gateway space station will
circle the Moon. Astronauts will stop
there on their way to the Moon
or Mars.

Voyager 1 and Voyager 2 have been in space for 45 years. They've gone 12 billion miles from Earth.

The James Webb Telescope is the most powerful space telescope ever. It took a photo of a group of galaxies 290 million light years away.

Glossary

billion (BIL-yuhn)—equal to 1,000 million

black hole (BLAK HOL)—an area of space with such a strong gravitational field that not even light can escape from it

dwarf planet (DWAHRF PLA-nuht)—an object in space similar to a planet but too small to clear other objects from its orbit

energy (EN-uhr-jee)—the ability to do work, such as moving things or giving heat or light

galaxy (GAL-uhk-see)—a large group of stars and planets

matter (MAT-ur)—particles of which everything in the universe is made

mission (MISH-uhn)—a planned job or task

supermassive (SOO-pur-mass-uhv)—very, very big

trillion (TRIL-yuhn)—equal to 1,000 billion

Read More

Gater, Will. *The Mysteries of the Universe: Discover the Best-Kept Secrets of Space*. New York: DK Children, 2020.

Labrecque, Ellen. *Mysteries of Meteors, Asteroids, and Comets*. North Mankato, MN: Capstone Press, 2021.

Lowery, Mike. *Everything Awesome About Space and Other Galactic Facts!* New York: Orchard Books, 2021.

Internet Sites

Cool Space Facts
planetsforkids.org/other/cool-space-facts.html#Information

Little Astronomy
littleastronomy.com

Passport to Space
kids.nationalgeographic.com/space

Index

About the Author

Ailynn Collins has written many books for children, from stories about aliens and monsters, to books about science, space, and the future. These are her favorite subjects. She has an MFA in writing for children and young adults from Hamline University and has spent many years as a teacher. She lives outside Seattle with her family and six dogs. When she's not writing, she enjoys participating in dog shows and dog sports.